THE KILLING OF A NATION - POLITICAL CORRECTNESS

WHEN EVIL BECOMES GOOD

Table of Contents

The Beginning of the End
    When Did the Demise Begin
Legal Issues
    The United States Constitution
    Free Speech
    Religion
    Pursuit of Happiness
    Second Amendment
Social Issues
    Education
    Colleges
    Parenting
    Racism
    Homosexuality
    Transgender
    Abortion
    Welfare
    Immigration
    Affirmative Action
    Feminism
    Sexual Harassment
    Military and Men and Women in Blue
    Media
    Global Warming
    War
    Israel
Ideologies
    Capitalism vs Socialism
    Liberalism
    Politically Correct Language
    Politically Correct History
    Christianity

In Conclusion
      When Evil Becomes Good
      Sin

INTRODUCTION

Anytime a nation succumbs to the ranting of the self-serving, immoral masses, it is on the demise. From the beginning of time, even Godless nations have realized there are rights and wrongs; and even though they may not have recognized God, they knew there was some kind of supreme power to which they were accountable. Of course, there have always been those in all civilizations through time that have totally defied right and wrong, and lived in chaotic darkness.

Even though the United States of America started out on a moral track, evil men with corrupt minds have tarnished the Red, White, and Blue; and instead of life, liberty, and the pursuit of happiness, man has become less free, placing himself in bondage to darkness. The more liberal a society becomes, the darker it becomes. Ideologies like "political correctness" contribute to such darkness.

All one has to do is look at history to see what became of once powerful nations who became   decadent and corrupt, i.e., Sodom and Gomorrah, the Babylonian Empire, the Assyrian Empire, the Roman Empire; and in more recent history, the Russian and German Empires. The United States is on a collision course with judgment, as well as the rest of the world, but I choose to focus on America's future; the elements that have led up to such a future; and what can be done, if anything, to change her course.

Who am I to write such a book. I am a middle-class American, the grassroots of America, one of the "deplorables", who has lived over 60 years, seen many things and experienced many things. I am not Ann Coulter, or Newt Gingrich, or Billy Graham; but I am a conservative American who can relate to the everyday man or woman. I could go into much more detail than what I have done, but I think you the reader will get the gist.

God has given me the idea to write this book and the ability to do so, as a blood-bought child of Jesus Christ. All honor praise and glory is His.

Sarah Wood-Bradford

Bible Acronyms:
KJV - King James Version
NIV - New International Version
AMP - Amplified
NLT - New Living Translation
AMPC - Amplified Bible, Classic Edition

The Beginning of the End

ONE

When did the demise begin?

Many may debate the time, but as a Baby Boomer, I will approach it from what I have seen in my lifetime, and what I know of history. Just as many know that the human body begins to die the minute it is born, the earth has been dying for thousands of years. Many in the medical community will admit that the minute you are born, you start losing brain cells. Some will attribute the earth dying to such things as "global warming". The truth, however, is that the physical body began dying upon birth after the original sin in the Garden. Sin is evil and eats away at the body like a cancer. In the same vein, the earth began dying upon original sin. Nature is negatively affected by sin just as the physical body is. Granted, man's lack of stewardship for his environment, which is sin, has contributed to its demise; but God is still in control, and man's moral degradation (sin) will influence when God decides to end it, not global warming, or whatever the environmentalists want to call it.

Throughout time many disasters have caused major destruction: such as volcanos, earthquakes, wars, floods, etc., but none when all of mankind has been destroyed. They have all been under the control of God. Did He cause all of them - no, but He allowed them to happen. We do know, however, He did bring the total destruction by flood in Noah's time because society was so morally decadent that He refused to allow them to live any longer. The only survivors were Noah, a righteous man in God's eyes, and his family, eight people in all; plus the animals that Noah was instructed to take on the boat. This disaster changed the whole makeup of the earth, climate changes and land formation changes.

Man was given a new start, but it didn't take long for the degradation to begin again. Thousands of years have passed. God is longsuffering but He will not always tolerate the immorality, the corruption, the perversion; all of which boils down to sin. As **Matthew 24:37** states, "As it was in the days of Noah, so it will be at the coming of the Son of Man."**(NIV)** Man is being warned that when society becomes so decadent as it was in the days of Noah, time is getting very short for this world.

What was going on in the days of Noah that made God angry enough to destroy civilization - for starters: thievery, murder, homosexuality, incest, bestiality, sodomy. Anything went and nothing was taboo. There was no respect for life. The same was going on in Sodom and Gomorrah later in history; and they were completely destroyed also, except for Lot and his family. **See Chapter 19 in the Book of Genesis.**

There has always been forms of decadence throughout the centuries, but not to the extent as was seen in the days of Noah and Sodom and Gomorrah...until the 21st century. Actually, we began to see this downhill spiral beginning in the 1960's. What was once morally unacceptable was beginning to be acceptable. God was becoming less of an influence. We started to hear the term "politically correct"; which previously was a term of which most people had never heard, two words that would become a destructive nightmare for our nation - **when evil began to be good**.

Legal Issues

TWO

The United States Constitution

In many circles the Constitution of the United States is considered to be obsolete. In recent years we have dealt with a slue of Supreme Court Justices who have read many things into the Constitution that are just not there; possibly to please the liberal masses, or be "politically correct". Either way, a great injustice has been done to the Constitution and to the individuals whose rights it was established to protect. The Supreme Court's job is to interpret law not to rewrite it or to make new law. Some decisions have been so radically out there that the end product in no form or fashion resembles the original clause or law.

The framers of the Constitution recognized that God (not Allah, not Buddha, not Muhammad) the Father, God the Son (Jesus Christ), and God the Holy Spirit was and is the Supreme Law of the land. They took into consideration His Truths when writing the Constitution. Some will argue that not all of the framers were Christians; maybe not, but they all recognized a Supreme Being that has Supreme control over the Universe. Today, however, many refuse to recognize this Power and Authority. However, that does not change the fact that God is still the Supreme Ruler, He is still in control; and they need to be forewarned that they should never become comfortable and think they have gotten by with something. God is longsuffering, but He also brings discipline and judgment in His time. God has blessed the United States; and when a nation and its people continue to abuse and ignore His commands, judgment will come.

THREE

Free Speech

"Congress shall make no law **respecting** an establishment of religion, or prohibiting the free exercise thereof; or abridging the freedom of speech, or of the press; or the right of the people peaceably to assemble, and to petition the Government for a redress of grievances."

I am going to concentrate on the freedom of speech clause for this section. In Chapter 8 on colleges I note the rhetoric of liberal professors. It is their right to teach it if the college allows it, and their right to speak it out to the public. It is my right to not listen to it and not have my children and grandchildren attend colleges that promote and support their rhetoric. If I want to fly a rebel flag in my yard, if I want to fly a rainbow flag, if I want to preach the truth of the Gospel that says homosexuality is a sin, under the Constitution that is my right.

<u>Double Standard</u>

However, what has happened is that some groups think it is their right to speak out their beliefs, but don't want the other groups they disagree with to have the same right. Good example - if a Christian group marches and stands on God's principles, coming against abortion and homosexuality, then you have such groups as the LBGT demanding that they be stopped. It is as much of a right for the Christian to make public their beliefs as it is for the LBGT groups to do so. It is not hate speech unless someone is threatened, just stating your belief and standing up for it is not hate speech. But, I have found that it is okay for the far left to protest and march, but not okay for the conservative right to do so. Such is a blatant violation of the Constitution and each individual's rights under the Freedom of Speech clause.

When free speech turns to violence, it is no longer covered under your First Amendment rights. Yes, the Ku Klux Klan (KKK) has just as much right to march as do Black Lives Matter (BLM), and Antifa. The problem is that Antifa promotes violence. That is not a right under the First Amendment. We have the right to "peaceably assemble". Because BLM does not like what the KKK stands for does not give them the right to beat up on them, or worse, and vice versa.

It has gotten out of control. Freedom of speech has been abused as has many other areas; and the Constitution loosely interpreted , if considered at all.

FOUR

"Religion"

As a pastor of mine said one time, "religion is either man's way of trying to get to God or man's way of trying to avoid God". "Religion" has been the cause of many wars, the cause of many people being deceived, and has helped to fulfill the purpose of Satan. It has become religiosity which is all about manmade doctrines designed to justify man's desires and lusts, and make him feel good about himself. Religion comes in all sizes, shapes, and denominations. Man's failure to seek out the Truth and instead placing his trust in manmade religion is sending many to Hell.

"Congress shall make no law respecting the establishment of religion, or prohibiting the free exercise thereof..." Two main issues have arisen that abuse this clause. Those that like to twist the constitution to suit their purposes, much like religions, say that public institutions cannot promote religion. Those are the people that railroaded the removal of prayer in schools. This constitutional clause was intended to prevent the government from establishing a state church like the early Americans had been subjected to under the Church of England. It was never intended to take God out of government. The authors of the Constitution and the Declaration of Independence recognized that God is the Supreme Law; and as such, constructed these documents to reflect the same. It has been and is the deviant powers that be that have distorted the religion clause.

More recently, groups have gone so far as to get prayer removed from school functions, the removal of inscriptions from pubic buildings that use the word God, and much more. The United States because of this clause has always been tolerant of the practicing of different religions, i.e, Buddhism, Hinduism, Islam, along with the mainstream religions. Now all of a sudden, the clause seems to apply to every religion except Christianity (which is technically not a religion which I will discuss later), and sometimes Judaism. We even have churches of Satan which doesn't seem to bother the liberals, but God does. Ironically, some schools don't have a problem with teaching the concepts of Islam, but would not think of discussing Christianity - the old double standard.

When evil becomes good...

FIVE

Pursuit of Happiness

Notice that one of the unalienable rights in the Declaration of Independence is pursuit of happiness; pursuit - going after it yourself, not the obligation of someone else to make you happy. Pursuit means that you need to make good choices in your life to obtain happiness. Socialism on the other hand tells us that those who work hard should divide what we have with those who don't have so that everyone has the same. Well, let's see how that works. I recently read in the news that socialist Venezuela is on the verge of collapse and people are fighting each other for food. They are starving. What happened to dividing everything equal so all would have the same. I guess someone didn't read the definition of socialism.

What happens is you have a working class, a working wealthy class, and then those that do nothing. So the working people are to divide their money with those who do nothing. Then working people think why should I work, I can still have the same as the others and not work. Before you know it, noone is working and the economy collapses. Let us not forget about some of those upper wealthy elites in those socialist countries. They are always spewing about the justice of a socialist form of government, which by the way some of our far left liberals would like to see happen; but somehow they keep their millions and dictate to the rest until the collapse, which the collapse always happens. Look at history.

The bottom line is that some will always have more than others, but we always have choices to rise above our circumstances and pursue that happiness whatever it may be. We don't have a right to happiness, but a right to pursue happiness.

SIX

Second Amendment

"...the right of the people to keep and bear arms **shall not be infringed**" - in case the liberals do not understand plain English, the word bear means to carry on the person. Owning and carrying a firearm on my person is my Constitutional right. States have overstepped their authority in making restrictive gun laws, by loosely interpreting the Constitution. Article VI of the United States Constitution prohibits such and maintains supremacy over the second amendment; however, the powers that be have dropped the ball and failed to assert their constitutional authority. Rather, they have allowed states to place unconstitutional restrictions on gun ownership.

The most recent mass killing at a school in Florida has raised the issue of gun restrictions again. Every time some such event happens, the Liberals raise their ugly heads and want to blame the guns. These killings are tragedies, but blame needs to be placed where blame is due. Guns don't kill, people do. Evil is prevalent in our society. When God takes a backseat in any society, evil will prevail. Evil people will always find a way to accomplish their wickedness no matter what laws are in place. Chicago has some of most restrictive gun laws in the country, but it has not stopped it from being one of the murder capitals of the country.

I read an article recently where a man in Indonesia attacked some people with a sword. With the mentality of some of our liberals, their recommendation would be to put a ban on swords - how idiotic. Lizzie Borden used an ax, the

Boston strangler used articles of clothing to strangle his victims, Jack the Ripper mainly used a knife; you should get my point.

When a government wants to take the weapons of its citizens, it wants to have total control over the people; and then they can do anything to the people they want. Look at history. Germany disarmed their citizens in the late 1930s, which allowed the Nazis to do their evil. Even Jesus knew that His people would need weapons to protect themselves from the evil. In **Luke 22:36,** He tells them if they do not have a sword, to sell some of their clothes and buy one.

When evil becomes good...

Social Issues

SEVEN

Education

The Banning of Prayer in Schools

On June 25th, 1962, the Supreme Court ruled that having prayer in schools was unconstitutional - 50+ years ago. Because of eight parents claiming that prayer in schools violated their constitutional rights to freedom of their beliefs (First Amendment), a whole nation was affected. The state courts had ruled that it was constitutional as long as it was voluntary, which it was; but the Supreme Court took the establishment clause to a whole new level, moving away from the intent of the original framers. When God is taken out of any equation, the equation loses functionality and disaster looms.

Corporal Punishment

Corporal Punishment has been banned in most states. However, approximately 19 states still use corporal punishment. Kudos to them. I live in Illinois, the liberal, financially broke state. You think they allow corporal punishment, not. Chicago alone had 789 homicides in 2016, and 679 homicides in 2017, a city full of juvenile murderers and other criminals. Fortunately, I live in downstate, but our public schools are affected by the liberal politics that come out of Chicago. I am retired, but I substitute teach fairly regularly in my district, which is small compared to some, but the discipline problems are out of hand. I have been threatened, cursed at; and police have been called to one of my classes to arrest a girl who dropped kicked a boy in the private parts and laid him out cold. Our high school and middle school have armed cops on duty at all times, plus a drug dog; and local police have to be called fairly regularly. We have Kindergartners who choke their teachers, head butt them, and stab them with objects. Local police have had to be called on elementary school students more than once. What they need is a good butt whipping. The teachers' hands are tied when it comes to discipline; the only avenues are in-house detention, suspension, or an "alternative school", which is a joke. We do have an alternative school that falls under another jurisdiction which operates quite well. It is very structured and is the last stop shop for many of these students before they are sent to juvenile lock-up. The students sent to this school, have a psychiatrist and/or a psychologist assigned to them; and some of them have parole officers. The district alternative school was opened last year because the state told them they had too many suspensions and had to provide an in-house option. Basically, the students are sent there for a few days for some infraction. They take work with them, but the structure is very lax. The troublemakers like going there because they don't have to do much but hang out.

I went to school in the 50's and 60's. The worst infractions did not even come close to what the educators deal with today. Why, because they were disciplined with a piece of wood early, and even in high school if necessary; and again by their parents when they got home. And, guess what, they didn't end up warped. They became productive, functioning individuals in society, not welfare, sucking, leeches; or punk gang bangers; or thieving, murdering jailbirds. Why don"t I say what I really think. Well, believe me, I am not done yet; and I am not menopausal. What I am is a well adjusted female who likes being female, the way God created me, living an orderly life through Jesus Christ; and I am sick and tired of seeing our children go down the tubes because of some liberal, destructive train of thought.

You say, how can a Christian think that way. Let me tell you what God says about discipline. "Whoever spares the rod, hates their children, but the one who loves their children is careful to discipline them." **Proverbs 13:24 (NIV)** "Foolishness is bound up in the heart of a child; the rod of discipline will remove it far from him." **Proverbs 22:15(NIV)** In case you haven't figured it out, the rod is some kind of paddle for a good butt whipping. If you belong to the group that says those Scriptures are Old Testament and don't apply today, see **Hebrews 12:7, 9-11**. There are many more Scriptures on discipline that you the reader can search out if you so choose. I will go into greater depth later about the welfare, sucking leeches and what the Bible says about them too - the entitlement mentality.

I have also taught in a Christian school. What a big difference. Most of these students know what the term respect means and they don't have near the amount of discipline problems that the public schools do. I know some of the Christian schools still use corporal punishment. Many times the Christian schools will have higher performing students also because the teachers can spend more time with the students, educating them rather than dealing with discipline and social issues.

Parent Responsibilities

I include parenting here because it has a lot to do with whether children succeed or fail in the educational system. There are a lot of good, responsible parents out there; but there are just as many or more that just donated some DNA. Teachers' jobs are supposed to be to teach reading, writing, math, science, social studies. Now they have to teach manners and hygiene, feed them, supply them with clothes and shoes, furnish them with school supplies; while their parents, parent, or custodial person uses their government money for drugs, alcohol, cigarettes, cable TV, cell phones (oh, excuse me, I forgot; under the Obama administration they got the cell phones free), etc. The only food that some of our children get is the breakfast and lunch the school provides them free. Many have no structure or discipline at home; thus, resulting in all kinds of behavior problems at school. Many are full of pent up anger, they are scared, they are not allowed to be kids. They go home to empty homes, not knowing when an adult will show up. Some deal with a parent's abusive partner. Some have been locked out of their home in the cold until late at night because the adult did not want to be bothered. Some have been molested by a parent and had a child by their father, living as if no big deal. Where is Social Services? You tell me. They won't let hard-working, middle-class families adopt a foster care child because the bedroom is not big enough, but they let them live with a "parent" who is a drug addict, and live in filth and neglect because they are with a "parent". I have seen everyone of these types of issues in the small school system in which I work. These issues transfer to the classroom. Many teachers have to spend classroom time away from actual teaching to deal with social issues. As a teacher, I can tell the kind of parenting a child is receiving at home by the way they conduct themselves at school.

At taxpayer expense, the schools have child psychologists, social workers, and child psychiatrists. You never heard of such when I or my children attended school. The school psychologist at one of our schools was a woman who became a man. Really??? She couldn't even come to terms with her own sexuality, but she is hired to counsel kids with problems. What an oxymoronic relationship.

Drugged Children

Some of the schools could be poster schools for how to drug your students into submission. It is really pathetic. There are behavior problems and then there are behavior problems. Some are just normal acting out for a child at a particular age which can be harnessed with proper parenting. The problem goes back to the parenting issue. Either you have no responsible custodian monitoring the child's behavior or you do have parents in the child's life, but they either have bought into the destructive ideas of Dr. Spock, or they are so consumed with themselves: make money, buy new house, have new cars; on and on, that technology becomes their children's babysitters and the children make their own rules and set their own structure as long as it does not inconvenience their parents. These are the self-centered children that come to school that expect the teachers to allow them to do the same things in the classroom they do at home, and have no respect for authority. The next step then is some so-called progressive medical person diagnoses them with ADD or ADHD, or one of the D's. They are then put on

drugs. I have seen worse behavior from some of these drugged up children than before they were put on them; so many side effects: can't stay awake in class, zombie like behavior; anger tantrums, excessive weight gain where they look like the Michelin Man. In many of the cases all they needed was some good structural parenting at home, consequences for inappropriate behavior, whether loss of privileges or an old fashioned butt whipping. Sadly, a lot of the teachers have bought into the medicating also. They are frustrated with their lack of discipline measures and having to deal with social problems with the students, they take the easy route and recommend medicine for children that show the slightest misbehavior. Neurologist and author Dr. Richard Saul in his book "ADHD Does Not Exist: The Truth About Attention Deficit and Hyperactivity Disorder" says it is a fake disorder and is a collection of symptoms, not a disease or disorder in itself. He goes on to say "parents seek an easy way to get their children to sit down and shut up, and the treatments for ADHD — Adderall and Ritalian — do the trick". It goes back to poor parenting, and some of the blame has to be placed on doctors who use this diagnosis so laxly and prescribe these medications.

There is a more sinister side to children being placed on these medications. It can provide an additional paycheck for the parents. Some parents, many already getting other government benefits, want their children to be diagnosed with this disorder so they can possibly get an additional check (SSI). It is always interesting to me to see all of the kids in one family who supposedly have this "disorder", and collect a check for each one - coincidence, or strategically planned? It really doesn't take much strategy to work this out when we have such an accommodating political system which easily gives free handouts, at taxpayer expense, for votes.

Political Correctness in the Schools

Teachers in the public schools have to be very careful not to talk about God or Jesus. I have had students ask me about God and some have never even heard of Jesus, sad. If they ask, I consider it fair game and answer what they want to know. Even though Christmas is about Christ - uh CHRISTmas, duh; the so-called school Christmas programs consist of "Jingle Bells", "Silver Bells", and the like. Once in a while they slip and put "Joy to the World" in there. When it comes to movie time at Christmas, a few teachers go ahead and show a Christian Christmas movie.

In one class I was teaching we played a spelling game to practice their spelling words. I gave the winner of each round a small prize. One of students asked why the rest of class didn't get something. I told them because they did not win. The response was that their other teacher always gave them something for participating. My response was that they need to realize in the real world not everyone gets a prize. If you participate in competitive sports like track, only the ones who do best get the prizes. You don't get a prize for participating. If you want a prize, you need to practice harder and maybe next time you will be the one to get a prize. It is not that you are a loser, but you did not meet the requirements to be best to get the prize. This is an example of some politically correct bull. If everyone gets a prize, where is the motivation to strive to do your best to reach a goal.

As of yet, our public schools have not had to deal with the transgender issue, in the sense of a big production about it. They are prepared; but nothing has arisen to date, one good thing about living in small rural Midwestern town, not the Bible Belt, but still has some morals and Godly attitudes.

We have those that like to be in the limelight in the upper grades and flaunt their affections with their same-sex partner. Of course, every place always has those that swim in a different stream.

Our schools still say the "Pledge of Allegiance", and have a moment of silence every morning to start the day. The High School has a Christian athlete group. Many schools are not even allowed to do this, or choose not to.

Teaching Time

Unfortunately, our teachers lose a lot of classroom teaching time. If they are not going to training sessions, they have to go to meetings with social workers, child psychologists, and child psychiatrists. As a result, the school district uses a lot of substitute teachers which adds to the budget. One plus is that our state requires substitute teachers to have at least a bachelors degree and they have to be certified. They are fingerprinted and have to pass a health physical. Some states only require a high school diploma and some use temp agencies to fill the openings.

Our state gives assessment exams three time a year. The first one is given right at the beginning of the school year to see how much the students have retained or forgotten over the summer. The second one is given either in December or first part of January to measure progress. The last one is given in the Spring, so about the last six weeks of school the teachers have to spend classroom time trying to prepare the students for these tests. The district looks more seriously at the Spring exam and bases teachers' job performance evaluations on how well their students do on this test, which is a flawed measurement. I have proctored these tests numerous times. Many factors play into the test results. Some students who do well overall in the classroom do not test well. Some students do not care and mark any answer just to get done. They know it does not reflect on their grades; and even if it did, many don't really care. Some that take it early in morning are tired, not awake yet, so they have a hard time focusing. On the other hand, some taking it later in afternoon are only thinking about going home. Many different factors affect the students' moods when taking these tests.   It is really unfair to the teachers to evaluate their performance based on such tests that have so many factors that affect the students' performance. Overall, I do not see that such tests are a good measure of the level at which each student is performing. Some states have gotten rid of these tests all together and others have greatly reduced the use of them.

Curriculum

Our state bought into the Common Core curriculum and was not smart enough to get rid of it like some other states did. Just in the few years I have been working with Common Core, I have seen a decline in student performance, especially in math. Whoever sold schools on this teaching method for math sure scammed them and saw them coming. For example: 3+7=10.   Normally, one would either memorize the fact or count out 3 of something and add 10 more. No, that would be too logical. Instead, this is what they do to first graders: count by threes until you get close to ten - 3, 6, 9, and how many more to 10 - add 1 more or 3, 6, 9, 12 - take 2 away to get 10. What kind of nonsense is this.

Teaching memorization has pretty much gone out the window. Many students in high school don't know their multiplication facts. They have to use a chart to tell them what 6x5 is; but yet they are teaching them algebra, which the majority of them will never use. Some teachers just let them use calculators, rather than make them figure it out for themselves. But, we all know what happens at the store when the computer goes down, many can't make change if they don't have the computer to tell them how much.

Many schools do not teach cursive anymore, my youngest Grandson's for one. His teacher writes the assignments on the board in cursive and a lot of it he cannot read. Our district does teach cursive, usually at the end of second into third grade. Cursive is not obsolete. In the adult world it is still widely used; but once again someone sold someone else on the idea that cursive was out of date. It would all be laughable if not so sad...and these people vote.

Some teachers do not spend much time on spelling, gotten rid of spelling tests. Many graduate out of high school and spell at a second grade level. I guess teaching students about "global warming", evolution, how to control your anger, films; and don't let us forget how to synergize, is more important than learning how to spell so you can fill out a job application. But, then having a job is not really that important when you have a government that will take care of you.

The "No Child Left Behind" program has put an extra financial burden on school districts, and has accomplished very little. According to learnthat.org, the United States ranks 49th out of 156 United Nations' countries in literacy. "More than half of America's secondary students struggle to read textbooks and other course materials." (learnthat.org) The research shows that most U.S. adults require at least two years of reading instruction just to become functionally literate, while the other alphabetic languages take about three months. So much for the "No Child Left Behind". The districts have had to add certified teachers to teach these Title reading classes, when most literate high school graduates could help these students with reading. Even my eighth grade Granddaughter could tutor in reading. Our district this year now is pulling out whole classes everyday for Title time, instead of just the low readers, at the expense of teaching Science and Social Studies; all to try to improve reading scores on the state tests. It has become all about those scores.

Grading System

The grading standards have been lowered. What used to be failing was anything below 70, now it is below 60. Instead of making students work to excel and meet certain standards, less is expected of them. Lower expectations produce lower performing individuals and affects the productivity of these individuals. What will be their contributions to society.

Summary

I did not retire from the public educational system; however, I have been teaching in some form or fashion for over 45 years. I have been teaching part time in the public school system for over 11 years. It is a sad scenario. With as high tech as our society has become, we are graduating dumber individuals. They cannot think for themselves, they have to rely on technology to think for them. Of course, there are exceptions, high performing students. These are the students that have good core values, have responsible parents/custodial people that take an interest in their education and work with them outside of the classroom environment. They are motivated and have goals.

There are still a lot of good teachers in the system trying to make a difference, but they are so limited by what they can do. They are told what to teach, when to teach it, and how to teach it. There is no room for their own creativity. Many of these programs they are required to teach are designed by people who never taught in a classroom; and a lot of the people telling them how to do their job have never taught in a classroom. If I still had school-age children, I would probably either find a legitimate Christian school or would home school. One of my Granddaughters has been home schooled from the beginning and is currently in the eighth grade. She is very advanced for her age. My daughter uses a very old curriculum teaching method. She has been reading Shakespeare since she was in the third grade, doing the usual Algebra that is taught in 8th grade, studying Spanish, typing, etc. She is very well-rounded. She has been taking various types of dance lessons since she was 3, so she is not isolated - very accomplished and competes nationally.

God instructed through His prophets that His people were to teach their children and their children's children the things of God, day and night, and to write it upon the tablets of their heart. We see what happened when later generations failed to do so. They became corrupt, deviant, ignorant, and many were destroyed. We live in a corrupt, deviant, ignorant society. The more high tech our society becomes, the dumber the people become. That is exactly what Satan wants. When you have ignorant people that cannot think for themselves, they are easier to control. What better way for him to accomplish it than through our children. He wants to program them young. You destroy a society when you start with the children and contaminate their minds. Many of the powers that be in our government know this, and that is what they want, a people that can be controlled. I will discuss this more later on.

EIGHT

Colleges

I know colleges fall into the category of education, but they deserve a chapter of their own. Many American colleges have become nothing more than a hotbed of Socialist, Marxist, Communist professors who are brainwashing our young with subversive doctrine; bent on destroying our Republic. It is appalling to hear some of the disgraceful, hateful rhetoric that hits the media from some of the so-called "elite" schools; some such schools having Christian beginnings, but have moved far from it. My undergraduate degree came from one of top schools in country. There were some liberal leanings then; more so when my oldest graduated from there. However, I was raised on a good foundation, as was she, so I was able to take it with a grain of salt and move on. Today there is more liberalism in these schools. Unfortunately, society is producing more enabled young adults that cannot think for themselves. They are being tutored by electronic devices and socialist oriented secondary schools, parents too busy with careers and/or too self absorbed to ground them. There are also many youngsters growing up in one parent or no parent families with no authority figure to teach and discipline. These groups are the most likely to fall prey to rhetoric being spewed by degenerate professors. Parents or custodians need to be very informed and aware of where they are allowing their children to go to college.

College sports have gone way over the line. I don't have anything against sports, but colleges are supposed to educate students to higher levels. Many colleges are more interested in their sports' teams than their academics. There used to be a concrete standard among the colleges for admitting students. Many now accept students that can barely read or spell because they can handle a ball. Many years ago my husband was visiting a college because he was in educational sales. They had classes to teach their students how to read and spell past an elementary level. How did they get admitted? I do have to say my undergraduate school may not be known for sports, but they are still one of the top schools in the country for an education.

It really is an insult to students who work really hard to get the grades and the money to go to college when some of their counterparts do neither, but get in because they can play a sport. There is something wrong with this picture. Very few of the sports' figures who actually make it to the pros, are successful in life after their sport's career ends. We read the stories all the time about the crimes in which many of them are involved, they fade away into obscurity. What was their contribution to the good of mankind.

NINE

Parenting

I talked some about parenting under education, but I want to talk about it in general also. Children are a gift from God. We don't own them, He loans them to us and expects us to train them and teach them to know Him. Part of that training is that as parents we are to discipline our children, and that includes spanking when necessary. **"He who spares his rod [of discipline] hates his son, but he who loves him disciplines diligently and punishes him early." Proverbs 13:24 (AMP)** Children like adults need structure and discipline. God disciplines His children. **"For the Lord corrects and disciplines everyone whom He loves and He punishes, even scourges, every son whom He accepts and welcomes to His heart and cherishes." Hebrews 12:6 (AMP)** I recently read that some woman in one of the states which I will not mention is proposing that spanking be outlawed - **when evil becomes good**.

I was spanked as a child and I spanked my own children. We are all well adjusted members of society. We know what it means to live by rules and be obedient. Many children today have no rules, they have no moral compass. We are starting to see the products of these types of children that are now becoming adults: no respect for anything; anything goes, instant gratification; self-centered; and no common sense. Anything less than obedience is sin.

God created the family. He created Eve to be a helpmate to Adam and gave them the ability to have children. He created each one to have their own role in the household.

They were created to be equal, not one superior to the other. Adam was created to be the protector of his family, the provider, and the spiritual leader. Eve was to be the nurturer of the children and to be in charge of running the home. Scripture tells us that the man is to love his wife as Christ loves the church. That is the agape type love which is a sacrificial, unconditional love; a choice to love even when the person is not always loveable. In return the wife is to respect her husband. There are many Scriptures in the Bible as to the roles of husband and wife. If each performs the roles as God intended, there is no conflict; no one being considered better or smarter than the other. The problem as many of us know is when we allow our sinful nature (our flesh) to get in the way, and then problems are created.

God never intended for there to be one-parent families. We see the societal problems that have been on the rise in recent years as one-parent families have become more of a norm rather than an exception. It used to be that one-parent families were attributed mostly to the death of one parent. Now it is more that babies are born out of wedlock and fathers just walk away. They really cannot even be called fathers, they only donated DNA. Even sadder though are those that plan to have children out of wedlock to collect a government check and have multiple children with multiple different men. There is no shame anymore to having a child out of wedlock, even though it is sin. It is not unforgivable; but the point is that people should not intentionally do so and make it a lifestyle. Everyone makes mistakes, sins, but the child of God recognizes that it is wrong and moves their life in another direction in line with God's commandments. As I mentioned above, God designed relationships, marriages between one man and one woman, and designed a role for each one. When one is absent and children are involved, those children miss out on the benefits of the one parent that is missing. Many of the crimes you see being committed today by young people are juveniles that have been raised in a one-parent family, especially the lack of a male authority figure. When the mother is the missing part, you see more emotional issues in those juveniles because one of the main functions of the mother is a nurturer. She teaches the children about emotions and feelings, more so than the father. Many one-parent families have done great jobs taking on the roles of both parents and the children have risen above the circumstances and become very productive members of society. However, there are many that don't.

On the other hand there are many two-parent families that don't function as parents. They are far removed from their children: self-centered, focused heavily on careers, children just being the thing to do. They can be families of considerable income, but basically the children raise themselves and are babysat by electronic devices or daycares. Some two-parent families can be dysfunctional because of addictions, abuse, or once again self-served interests; just like one parent families.

Whichever is the case, the children of these types of parenting scenarios suffer. As I previously mentioned, some rise above their circumstances through sheer determination and will. Sadly others become the same type of parents, while others live a defeated, sometimes tragic life.

God takes parenting seriously. He is the creator, and each child whether planned or not, is one of His special creation. Parents will be held accountable to Him on the job they did, and will be judged accordingly on Judgment Day when they stand before the Judgment Seat of Christ.

TEN

Racism

Every time you turn around, someone is playing the race card; and it is usually the blacks playing it. Now call me racist for saying that. Look at BLM. It is always about race and it is all the white people's fault. The white liberals like to play the race card to either garner votes if they are in the political arena or they are the people trying to impress someone to get attention. Racism has been around for thousands of years so it is not a 17th, 18th, 19th, 20th, or 21st century concept.

I am so tired of hearing about the poor, put upon blacks. Everything bad that happens to them is because they are black, they are not treated fairly, they don't have the same advantages, they are profiled; and on and on and on. Well, news flash in case you haven't read previous reports; this is the 21st century and even if you can trace your relatives back to slaves, that is not you. And if I traced my relatives back to someone who owned slaves, that was them and not me. Even back then it was not all the white man's fault. Some of your "relatives" in Africa weeded out the ones in their tribes they felt were inferior and sold them to the white man. So, get over yourselves, move on, and quit blaming someone else for your problems.

In the course of history I believe the Israelite people have experienced the most racism. Whether you read Biblical or secular history, you will find that many times before Christ the Israelite people were enslaved. We all know what Hitler did to millions of them. I believe that was pretty racist. We still have groups today that are blatantly racist against the Israelite people. Have they or do they constantly complain about the prejudices against them and expect someone else to give them handouts and special treatment because they are Israelites. I don't think so. As a matter of fact, many that lost everything to the Nazis and got out before Hitler destroyed them came to the United States and became thriving members of society. Some that survived concentration camps made it to the United States, some stayed in Germany or surrounding countries and became productive members of society. They did not constantly bring up the injustice and expect special treatment from the rest. They blamed who was responsible, not generations to come or a particular race. Their relatives today don't expect any payout or special treatment because of what happened to their families years ago.

What about the Japanese? There were many Japanese families in the United States during World War II that were rounded up and interred in camps and their property confiscated. Many of these families were American citizens, and some had been born in the United States; but because of what happened at Pearl Harbor, they were "profiled". When the war was over and the camps were closed, these people assimilated back into the American culture, went to work, became productive members of society, not playing the race card because they were and are Japanese.

Who more in the United States than the Native American Indian knows about racism. Almost from the beginning that America began being settled by other countries, has the Native American Indian been persecuted and has experienced the consequences of racism. Even today in this country, there are areas that are highly prejudiced against this race. But, they are not always playing the race card.

I live in the Midwest, in fairly close proximity to Ferguson, Missouri. Well, I think most of the nation is familiar with the fiasco that happened there. Once again the race card was played; poor, innocent black kid killed by a white cop. He was not an innocent kid. He was a thug, had recently committed a robbery, and had a criminal history. Then the morons in the persons of Jesse Jackson and Al Sharpton show up to add fuel to the fire, more race cards. It was proven that a lot of the people doing the protesting were paid people that were not even from that area. Not only did they protest, but they destroyed millions of dollars of property. There were hard working black people who were caught in the fracas and had their businesses destroyed. This is not justice. This is a bunch of thugs trying to bring attention to themselves in the guise of coming against racism, when all they were interested in doing was to capitalize on the misery of others. These people have done this time and again across the country.

What happens when a white person, or an Asian person, or a Jewish person gets killed by a cop, and yes sometimes it is a black cop who does the killing? Do you see their groups take to the streets, declaring racism, and them destroying property. I don't think so. The ones always playing the race card are themselves being racist when they want to blame everything on the white person or some other race. Every race has experienced racism at some time or another. Yes, racism is a sin, but destroying people's property, and doing violence to someone's person is a sin also. So, "Rev", Jackson, try explaining all your actions to God. Get over yourselves, move forward. Look at Dr. Ben Carson. He was not raised in the height of wealth, quite the opposite. He had a mother who instilled in him good work ethics, a good foundation; and she never doubted that he could succeed. She never claimed being black would keep her children from succeeding. He is a good Christian man who is a credit to our country. Every person is given opportunities of some kind. We choose to either take them or to wallow in the mire. It is our choice and we cannot hold our color or anyone else to blame. We choose to rise above our circumstances or to sink even lower.

It is sad because people like Dr. Martin Luther King worked hard and lost his life trying to bridge the gap between the races. Today, however, the gap has widened to a point wider than it has been in many, many years. What makes it even sadder, is that the people widening it are taking advantage of the ignorance of those they claim to be supporting. They are doing it for personal gain and to cause division. Satan is good at using people to accomplish his goals. Division is one of the ways he causes destruction. As **St. Mark 3:25** states, "And if a house be divided against itself, that house cannot stand."**(KJV)** The masses are being duped by puppets of Satan, and he is having a field day - **when evil becomes good**.

ELEVEN

Homosexuality

I was in high school in the late 60's. I had never even heard the term homosexuality. The most I knew about this perversion (it was not considered a lifestyle then) was some chatter amongst us teenagers about a couple people in our local area who preferred sexual relations with people of their own sex. We used the term queer. It was not really a topic we discussed much other than in passing every once in a while for a snicker.

That was almost 50 years ago, what a change, not one for the better. **Leviticus 18:22** says, "Thou shalt not lie with mankind, as with womankind: it is an abomination."**(KJV)** These are God's words. If you want them in modern language, men are not to lie with men and women are not to lie with women.   This is only one of the Scriptures in the Old Testament that addresses the issue of homosexuality and there is more than one in the New Testament also. In **Romans 1:26-28,** God through St. Paul is talking about how evil the world is becoming and how God has just turned them over to their "vile affections...", "for even their women did change the natural use into that which is against nature: And like wise also the men, leaving the natural use of the woman, burned in their lust one toward another; men with men working that which is unseemly and receiving in themselves that recompense of their error which was meet...." **(KJV)**

Homosexuality is not a disease. People are not born homosexual. God did not make any mistakes. Homosexuality

42

is a choice. God would never condemn anything that a person had no control over, and the Bible is very clear that He condemns homosexuality, it is sin. No matter that society says it is an alternative lifestyle, God's Law is Supreme. "For the Lord your God is God of gods, and Lord of lords, the great God, mighty and awesome, who shows no partiality and accepts no bribes." **Deuteronomy 10:17 (NIV)** God does not change, His precepts remain for ever and ever. "For I am the Lord, I change not..." **Malachi 3:6 (KJV)**

I am not here to condemn those who choose to live this type of lifestyle. God will hold each person accountable for the way they lived their lives. We all will stand before the judgment seat of Christ. "For we must all appear before the judgment seat of Christ; that every one may receive the things done in his body, according to that he hath done, whether it be good or bad." **II Corinthians 5:10 (KJV)** My point in bringing up this subject is that my right to pursuit of happiness and to practice my beliefs are being infringed upon when this lifestyle is constantly thrown in my face and shoved down my throat. If homosexuals want to live the lifestyle, fine; but don't expect that lifestyle to be taught in the public schools. The public schools don't teach about Jesus Christ as Lord and Savior so why do some homosexuals think the schools should teach about homosexuality.

Under the Freedom of Speech clause, I have as much right to march in disapproval of homosexuality as homosexuals do to march in favor of it or in disfavor of how Christians think on the subject, as long as the language does not become threatening or the people become physical against another person. Peacefully assemble - some people have a problem doing so.

TWELVE

Transgender

Once again, God does not make mistakes. His creation is perfect. Man through his sin has caused many things to go awry. "Male and female created he them..." **Genesis 5:2 (KJV)** If someone is born male and feels he should be female, or vice versa; that is that person's own twisted thinking. God did not cause that nor does He condone it. Schools should not be required to recognize such, having birthed females go to male restrooms because they feel like a male, males going to female restrooms because they feel like a female. For such a supposedly intelligent society; stop and think how stupid this sounds, but yet it is being done. Have a unisex bathroom for those people and they all can congregate together and decide who is who. Why should my children or grandchildren be exposed to such perversity. And, that is what it is, perversion. Thankfully my children are raised because they would not attend a school that allowed such. Thus far my grandchildren who attend public schools have not been exposed to it. There is something to be said about living in smaller areas of the Midwest. We still have some morals and principles. One of my other grandchildren is home schooled and another goes to a private school so there are no issues there.

It is one thing for an adult to change his or her sex. They are responsible for themselves, but a minor? What kind of parents allow such nonsense. Of course the term parent is used loosely today, more like they just donated some DNA.

God blesses people with their children, but they are on loan to us. When He blesses us with children, we are expected to be good stewards of them and raise them according to His principles, and to know Him. Parents will be held accountable for the job they did with their children when they stand before Him in judgment. When He calls them on letting a child determine their own sex, it will be interesting to see how they try to justify themselves.

However, I recently read in the news that a court removed the child (minor) from its home because the parents would not agree to sex change treatments - **when evil becomes good**.

THIRTEEN

Abortion

According to the Declaration of Independence, all human beings have three unalienable rights given to them by their Creator: life, liberty, and the pursuit of happiness. The authors of this document thought it the duty of the leaders of the nation to ensure that these rights were protected for each individual. When it comes to abortion, the crux of the matter is when does life begin. For a child of God, a Christian (one who has put their trust and faith in Jesus Christ and made Him Lord of their life); knows, or should know, that life begins at conception. "Before I formed thee in the belly I knew thee; and before thou camest forth out of the womb I sanctified thee..." **Jeremiah 1:5 (KJV)** This is God speaking. He knows each person before they begin to form. He has a plan and purpose for their life. "For thou hast possessed my reins; thou hast covered me in my mother's womb." **Psalms 139:13(KJV)**

Who protects the life of the unborn. Since the decision of *Roe v. Wade*, the unborn became fair game. It is downright murder. It does not matter that our laws allow it, God's law calls it murder and His Law is Supreme. The number of abortions in the United States every year is staggering. Each year the numbers are in the hundreds of thousands. You can go to jail for killing an animal, but not for aborting a baby. How does that work? - **when evil becomes good**.

Is it more humane to abort a baby in the first three months than it is after that. Whether it is more humane or not, it is still murder, a life is being taken.

If a woman does not want to have a baby, then she needs to keep her legs closed or use a reliable method of birth control. There is no excuse. Even if the woman is raped, there is no excuse to abort a baby. The baby is still a creation of God. There are thousands of parents who would love to adopt a baby, so if you are pregnant and don't want the baby, put the baby up for adoption. You might even find someone to pay you to have the baby, if you want to capitalize on it.

Think of how many geniuses, doctors, scientists, artists, missionaries, mothers, fathers, have been aborted. My oldest daughter was by a man who didn't not want to have a child. He wanted me to have an abortion. That was before abortions were legal. The legality of if was not a consideration for me because I never considered it an option. I ended up having her without any kind of support from him, physically, emotionally, or financially. He skipped out, even left the country for a period of time to avoid paying child support. That was a relationship in name only. He donated DNA, but was never a father. The love of God sustained me through it all and I ended up marrying a man that raised her as his own, never any differences between her and our other children. That child today is an amazing Pastor who has touched many lives. Think of the people that would have been deprived of the gifts that God has given her. Think of what God would have said to me on judgment day when He called me on killing His anointed.

I know of women who have spent their lives with guilt over aborting a baby. It is not an unforgivable sin, but for it to be forgivable you have to have a relationship with Jesus Christ. Even after repenting and turning to Jesus Christ, many of these women still have a hard time letting go of the bad decision they made. Most women I believe, even if they would not admit it, are haunted in some form or fashion by such a decision. But, then you will always have those women that are so cold and detached (evil is the word), that has no conscience about it at all.

Once again the government stuck their nose into something they had no business doing so. Abortion is not new to society. It has been around for thousands of years. Our great, great, great, great (more greats then we can count) grandmothers used more than one kind of method to rid themselves of unwanted children. It didn't make it any more right then, than how it is done today, but they didn't need the government regulating it.

Why do I as a taxpayer have to have a portion of my taxes go to a procedure that goes against my beliefs. There is something wrong with that picture. My state, which is already broke, voted recently that taxpayers have to help fund abortions. If women want abortions, they need to be able to pay for it themselves. This law violates my First Amendment rights.

FOURTEEN

Welfare

I am talking about paying people not to work, Medicaid, Welfare, whatever title you want to give it. What a joke, what a drain on the system, what a vote getter. Why do you think the Democrats are the welfare party. They don't care about these people, free money will get them votes.

In the 1930's Franklin Roosevelt was instrumental in establishing the WPA, a program to put unemployed people to work and to give them financial assistance until they could get back on their feet. I have always credited this program with the start of welfare. My husband who is considerably older than I thinks it was a good program with good intentions. He would have been a child at that time. The intent might have been good, the problem is that somewhere along the line the financial assistance from the government continued, but the working stopped. When the government gets involved in such areas of people's lives, it becomes out of control. It becomes about politics and power rather than the good of the people. The welfare program really started to expand in the 1960's under the Kennedy and Johnson administrations. It is out of control.

It is hard to even know where to begin on this subject. But, I am going to begin with what the Bible says, and God's Word trumps everything else. In **II Thessalonians 3:10(KJV)**, God speaking through Paul says, "...if any would not work, neither should he eat." That is quite clear. The Bible does make provisions for widow and orphans. In **I Timothy 5:3-16** it is very clear on what classifies one as a widow that the church would support. Besides having lost her spouse, she would have no kin. The Bible states that kin like children and nephews are responsible first for providing for her needs. It goes on to state that she has to have a relationship with the Lord; in other words, having accepted Jesus Christ as Lord and Savior, walking in obedience to the Lord, and being an active part of the church body. Orphans would be any minor that does not have close family to provide for them. **James 1:27** also mentions providing for orphans and widows. Granted, many churches go beyond and help out individuals and families in the community outside of their body. However, their first responsible is to their Brothers and Sisters in Christ, and especially to the ones in their own body of worship. In churches over the years to which I have belonged, we have helped countless people pay house payments, utility bills, bought groceries and clothes for them. Not all of them were a part of our church, but they were in need. We participate in Salvation Army Christmas drives, local food pantries, Samaritan's Purse, etc. We have had people in our church body that live off of a government welfare check, could work, and are always whining about being out of food or having no gas money. They buy cigarettes, soda, potato chips. No, we don't help them. I will go into more detail about this issue farther down. God created us to work. God worked six days when He was putting together creation. He rested on the seventh. As a child, I remember my mother saying, "if the corn isn't shelled, drive on". It took me some years to figure out what that saying meant. In the Bible it talks about gleaning. After a field was harvested, the master of the land would allow the servants to come into the field and collect any left over grain in the field and have it for their personal use. My father was a farmer. In his day corn was picked by ears and not shelled ahead of time. Just like today the picker would miss or drop some ears on the ground. My father would allow a neighboring family who were workers, but poor, come in and glean the fields for dropped ears to use for their personal needs. The saying means that some people are so lazy that unless the corn is already shelled for them, they will not take it because they will have to shell it themselves. Some people that live on Welfare have the same mentality. They feel entitled to a check they have not earned and are not willing to do anything for it. I know of people who go to the food pantry for the free food, but will only take the food that does not require preparation. **Proverbs 26:15(NLT) says, "Lazy people take food in their hand but don't even lift it to their mouth".**

There are many facets of Welfare. One of the programs is SSI. One politician had the audacity to call Seniors who are drawing off of their Social Security, greedy, because they were upset that cuts were going to be made. Excuse me. We are the working class who have paid into the system for decades. It is our right to collect out of it. I have paid into Social Security since I was 14. It is easy for a politician who never pays into the program and still lives off of the taxpayer after they leave office to use the Seniors as scapegoats to blame for the program having funding issues. You politicians are the ones who have stolen money out of the program to use for things for which it was never intended. One such program is SSI. SSI was set up to provide financial assistance to the disabled. The problem is the term disabled has taken on a whole new meaning over the years. One of the biggest scams are people having a doctor diagnose their children with "behavior" problems: ADD, ADHD, bipolar, manic depressive, autism, and the list goes on. Many doctors seem to be quite loose with the ADD and ADHD diagnoses, shame on them. Many of these kids just need structure and discipline, and maybe an old fashioned butt whipping.   The parent or parents get a check for these children because they are deemed disabled. I know families that are collecting such checks for three and four children. It is a racket. The money comes out of the Social Security program, a program that they have not paid any money into to cover these children. I happened to have a career from which I retired that did not pay into Social Security, only Medicare, because we had our own retirement system. I had worked enough before that job and paid into Social Security to quality me for Social Security benefits. However, my benefits are greatly reduced because of my retirement salary. Before my first husband died, he collected Social Security. He had paid a large amount into the program because of the salary he made; but when it came time for him to collect, he was docked because I was still working and making good money. Why should my salary have anything to do with his, he paid the money to the program. And then to add insult to energy, we have to pay taxes on the benefits each year. Yet, we have those collecting the benefits that have never paid a dime into it. So, who is breaking the system?

Then there are Food Stamps, LINC cards, or whatever each state calls them. A lot of the recipients were selling the stamps to have cash to buy things the stamps would not allow, including illicit drugs, so they changed to cards. Now they just sell the cards. If people need to have such assistance, their should be strict limitations on what can be bought with these cards. It should be items like fresh meat, fruit, vegetables, and basic staples like rice, beans, etc. Exclusions should be such items as pizza rolls, frozen dinners, potato chips, cookies; and no they don't need to go to the seafood market and buy shrimp and the such with the government card. A lot of working people cannot afford these foods. If you want to buy steak and shrimp, then get a job.

My husband stood behind a lady at the courtesy counter at a local grocery and watched her cash $9,000 worth of government checks for one month. He mentioned it to the clerk and she told him that is only the tip of the iceberg.

Many of the students I have taught have families that live on government assistance, but yet the only meals these children get are the breakfasts and lunches the schools serve them because their custodians are buying cigarettes, alcohol, and drugs. They have cell phones and cable or satellite TV. They don't work, and they are in the age category of 25-45 with no disability. Then, of course, we have the teen mothers that live off of the system also. If you need a welfare check, you don't need a cell phone, you don't need cigarettes, alcohol, or drugs, you don't need cable or satellite TV; and your kids don't need free meals at school. One of the sad things is that the children that live like this will in all likelihood live this way as adults. Very few will become productive members of society, they will perpetuate this way of living and feel entitled to it.

The government, politicians, have created an entitlement mentality in these people. Many support it because it gets them votes. In actuality these people living off of the government are in bondage, they are enslaved and controlled by the government. Those trying to move this nation to Socialism want this because they want to control the people.

What happens to a nation when the welfare population outnumbers the working population? If you take into consideration those retired and the welfare population, the percentage already is not that far off of the working population. Without a stable workforce, eventually the economy will collapse, government will shut down, and there will be chaos because those used to living on handouts will take to the streets to try to take from those who still have something.

What is wrong with drug testing welfare recipients? Many workplaces drug test, and you are out of a job if you test positive. The taxpayer is funding a lot of recipients' drug habits. Every month they should be tested before they receive any assistance. A lot of states have proposed such laws; but as of this writing, nothing has happened. Too many politicians are afraid it would cost them votes.

What about population control if they want to receive government assistance - limit one kid and after that you are on your own, no increase in benefits. Very few states have a cap for number of children and those that do have a lot of wiggle room for exceptions. The bleeding hearts argue that this approach would not stop people having kids, but add kids that would go hungry. That is flawed thinking. Once those recipients know they are not going to get more money for more kids, they will not have more kids because they are not interested in the kids anyhow. They just want more money. As I mentioned earlier, a lot of these kids are hungry and neglected anyhow because their custodians are not using their assistance on them but themselves. These kids should be taken out of these homes and put up for adoption. The states put out a lot of money for foster parents anyhow, better than giving the money to worthless parents; open the door to adoption without a lot of restrictions. Welfare has become a business for many families; and I use the term family loosely - cats have a better family unit; keep having those babies with many baby daddies and let the checks roll in. Like one of my Pastors said one time, Father's Day must be real interesting for some of these people.

Medicaid - public financed healthcare, another drain on the economy and the taxpayer. Many years ago before I began my professional career I worked in the healthcare industry. The healthcare facility served a community of about 8,000 people plus surrounding rural areas. The young medicaid recipients would come into the emergency room on a regular basis for such minor things as a headache, menstrual cramps, stubbed toe, etc. They could not go to a doctor's office because doctors in the area would not take medicaid because of how long it took for them to get their money. But why do you need to see a doctor for these things anyhow. It is real easy to just go to the ER when you are not paying for it and believe me some made sure to tell you they did not have to pay anything, with no sense of shame.

On the other hand, we had aged patients come in that were inpatients that really needed care. Some of them really needed the medicaid but there was a catch for them. They had worked all their lives at jobs with lower wages, saved up enough money to buy a home; but only had Social Security on which to rely . They did not collect much Social Security because they never earned much money. Now they are up in years, starting to have health issues, and dealing with Medicare. Well Medicare does not pay everything. They don't have enough money to pay the premium on a supplemental policy, and the only way they can quality for Medicaid is to turn their home over to the state. They can stay in their home, but when they die, it becomes the property of the state. A lot of these elderly people chose to keep their homes and faithfully came in every month to make some kind of payment on their bill. But yet we have the lazy, do nothings I mentioned above that do not work, have never worked, and get their medical care basically free. What kind of justice is this?

You can live on less. I have been there and done that. In my early married life in the 1970's, I had two children under the age of 2. My husband was paid weekly. After we paid the bills, we usually had about $10 left each week for groceries. Granted, prices were cheaper then, but that was not much for groceries. I made sure the children had milk, we had bread and eggs, and I would buy a weeks worth of ground beef to last until the next paycheck. Ground beef was fairly cheap then. Sometimes I might have some zucchini out of my in-laws garden if they were in town (they lived out of state). We lived on ground beef with salt and pepper and zucchini for quite some time. Sometimes I might have a can of tomatoes, whatever was cheap, that I could buy to flavor the ground beef. Sometimes it was browned ground beef with salt and pepper only. I made sure the children had some fruits and vegetables and oatmeal. We did not use WICK, if it was around then. We did not have food stamps or any other government assistance. It did not even enter our mind to look into government assistance. We were taught to work and that family takes care of family as needed. A living is not a right, it is a privilege.

FIFTEEN

Immigration

As the 19th century moved into the 20th century, the United States began seeing a large influx of immigrants coming into the country. Many coming in were from such countries as Italy, Ireland, Poland, Hungary, and so on. In the early 1900's most of these immigrants were routed through Ellis Island. If they were deemed to be criminals or carrying disease, they were shipped back to their home country at the expense of the shipping line. They were asked if they had money to live on, a job, etc. The government was not going to take care of them. These many different cultures worked hard and helped to make the United States great. They were not looking for a free handout. They assimilated into American culture, learned to speak English. Many lived in poverty, low wages, but they worked wherever they could find it. They did not live off of the government. They embraced the American way of life, saluted the flag, served in the military, and fought its wars.

The Constitution provides that someone who wants to become a citizen, must have established a **legal** residency, must take an oath of allegiance to the United States, be able to pass some exams, be able to read, write, and speak English, and be of good moral character.

What is happening today not only violates the Constitution but is an insult to all those immigrants in the past who have come here legally and gone through the proper channels to become a citizen.

Once again we see politicians willing to allow anything to get votes. What happened to enforcing the law - **when evil becomes good**. If they are not here legally, no matter how you slice it they are criminals. We don't need them as workers. We have plenty of our own workers, but many employers that use them want cheap labor and are not concerned whether or not they are here legally.   Many are getting welfare checks from the government and free medical care when some of our own hard working citizens don't get the same. They want to protest and fly their country's flag in our face. If their country was so great where they still want to honor that flag, then they need to go back there. We don't need or want you here with that attitude, and especially if you are here illegally. Many are criminals of all kind. How many murders are being committed by illegal aliens. How many drug dealers and drug crimes are perpetrated by illegal aliens. A report just came out as of this writing that more crimes are committed by illegals than by our citizens. They cost the taxpayer in court costs, prison care, medical care, and on and on; and how much of the money of those that actually work stays in this country. They are an abscess on our nation. Why should they be granted amnesty. They need to go back to their country and enter legally and go through the proper legal procedures to become a citizen. Being a citizen is a privilege, not a right; and with it comes responsibilities.

Law enforcement rounds up child molesters, women molesters, murderers, thieves, drunken drivers; so round up the illegal aliens and send them back. They are law breakers also. Yes, build the wall, beef up border patrol, fine employers who employ the illegals, fine the cities and states who harbor them and refuse to comply with the law, remove some of their grant monies. What gives them the right to think they are above the law - **when evil becomes good**.

The 14th Amendment has been taken way out of context and stretched far beyond what was intended. This travesty should come as no surprise to many of us. The unscrupulous and self-serving, power-hungry administrators of this country, and states and cities, adjust the Constitution and many other laws to suit their personal purposes - **when evil becomes good**.

SIXTEEN

Affirmative Action

Affirmative action is receiving special treatment without earning it. Affirmative action is getting accepted to a college because of your race or gender, not because of your academic achievements. It has happened at many of the top elite universities who turn down high scoring students, or not quite the highest; but accept ones that could barely make it into a Junior college, because of their race more so than their gender. This idea is once again rewarding the slackers and penalizing the workers. Why does there have to be a certain number of each race on the enrollment. The enrollment should be based on the highest achievers.

Medical school is darn hard to get into anyhow. The schools limit their numbers, but they do the same thing. They want to meet a quota on race and gender. I am glad to see in recent years that many entities have done away with affirmative action. Government employers had to implement affirmative action. I worked for a state government agency. I handled all of this agency's contracts. The agency received federal grant monies as well as state funds. When selecting a contractor for specific work, we had to pay special attention to companies that were minority owned (women or minority race).

When my son-in-law got out of the military, he applied for a job with the Postal Service. Supposedly veterans were supposed to get extra points for hiring on their ratings. But, guess what, the minority races received more rating points than a veteran. What kind of crap is that. A person who has served their country is rated lower than someone whose only qualification is their race.

My deceased previous husband worked for ten years in heavy equipment construction. Because the company did a lot of contract work for the state, they were required to hire a certain number of women and/or minority races. Apparently the minority races were not interested in that kind of physical labor at that time but they did hire some women. The women did not have the physical strength to operate the large equipment used in the construction of bridges and roads, so they were put on the jobs like holding the signs. I do remember, however, there was one woman during that ten-year period that was as tough as nails and she could operate those machines with the best of the men. That was not the norm, but the exception. The next time you are stopped in traffic for construction, take a look at the sign holders and the equipment operators, and take note of what you see. There are just some jobs that women do not have the physical strength to do. It has nothing to do with their intelligence. God did create men to be physically stronger than women. There are always exceptions.

Standards should not be lowered to accommodate any particular group of people. If the person can do the job based on what is normally expected for that job, then fine. People should be rewarded for hard work and a job well done, not for the color of their skin or their gender. God is not going to accept people into heaven because they were a minority here on earth or because they were a female. He will not look at what religious affiliation you had. Your admittance to heaven will be based solely on whether you accepted His son Jesus Christ as your Lord and Savior and you put your total trust and faith in Him. If you pass that test, then Jesus will judge you and pass out your rewards based on what works you did that furthered His Kingdom and brought Him glory. **John 14:6** says, [Jesus speaking], "I am the way, the truth, and the life: no man cometh unto the Father, but by me." (KJV) II Corinthians 5:10, "For we must all appear before the judgment seat of Christ; that every one may receive the things done in his body, according to that he hath done, whether it be good or bad." (KJV)

SEVENTEEN

Feminism

I agree that women doing the same jobs should get the same pay as men. However, one of the problems has been when females have been put in jobs they are not physically capable of doing, but are placed there to fulfill a quota for affirmative action like I talked about previously. Being hired and staying hired should be based solely on job qualifications and performance, nothing else.

Some of the women wanna be men or just want to make a statement, diss men for being respectful to them. I like being a woman and I like a man showing me extra courtesies like opening the door for me and seating me at the table or standing while I seat myself. That is good manners, not a man treating a woman as a lesser person. Now if you as a woman don't like those courtesies, fine; but don't consider me weak because I do. I had a career in an area where most of the other professionals were men, I was the boss of a lot of them. My salary was equitable and I never felt there was a man/woman issue. Now I know that isn't the case with all places.

The problem with some of these platforms like Feminism is that the extremists take it way too far and give others a bad name. Great strides have been made, but I know there are some discrepancies in pay at some jobs. The solution is either to not work there, or stay the course and try to get it changed. Don't define me or someone else who is comfortable in their skin and with how they are treated.

EIGHTEEN

Sexual Harassment

Women nor men should have to tolerate being sexually harassed. It is not just a one-sided issue. Maybe 65 or so years ago it may not have been an issue with men being sexually harassed; but with the sexual revolution and feminism men became fair game also. I don't think you hear about it as much with the men because I believe they are more embarrassed to admit that a female has sexually harassed them - a male ego thing. However, since the LGBT have come out of the closet, the sexual harassment covers many different types of scenarios.

Periodically we have heard about a high profile sexual harassment case, but in the last few months the news has been flooded with such cases. The issue I have with many of these cases is the numbers of years that have passed before the incidents are reported. Now everyone is jumping on the bandwagon. It is apparent that some were let go because the ones being harassed were more interested in what it might do to their career at the time than having justice done. Now when the supposed harasser can no longer do anything for them, they get media attention by bringing it to light. I am not suggesting that the perpetrators get off scot free, but I have no respect for a woman or man who lets such behavior continue rather than risk their careers. They are opportunists until the opportunities are no longer there, and then they cry wolf.

NINETEEN

Military and Men and Women in Blue

It is such a travesty how these two groups of people are treated today. The Military are those men and women who protect this country at home and internationally. They sacrifice time with their families and many times their lives to protect our freedom. Their pay is minimal compared to a lot of other jobs that don't come close to performing the great service they do. Look at professional athletes and actors. I don't consider athletes and actors as doing a service for me or my country. They can be entertainment, but in the scheme of things, what are these two professions really worth. Some of the idiotic, stupid things that come out of their mouths really remind me how little, if any, contribution they make to society. A lot of welfare recipients make more money for doing nothing, than what our military people make.

Many of our veterans come home disabled, really disabled. They have a hard time getting appropriate medical treatment, and their families struggle to make ends meet because of the lack of benefits.

Our men and women in blue are treated like they are the criminals because they are doing their job. They walk around with targets on their backs, and all the officials want to do is be politically correct and hold up for the criminal. Granted there are and always will be some bad apples, but for the most part the Blue are trying to keep our streets and neighborhoods safe. A lot of these city neighborhoods across the country need a lot more taken out instead of wasting taxpayer money on them in the court and prison system.   The

Blue need to have more metals pinned on them for ridding our society of the scum. Chicago and Philadelphia need to take a lesson, but then they need some leadership change also.

These are prime examples of **WHEN EVIL BECOMES GOOD**.

TWENTY

Media

That word has almost become a curse word. Granted we use the term media to describe our electronic devices like iPads, cell phones, PCs, etc. I am referring to the so-called news media or sadly to say the gossip reporters and the liars. What happened to true reporters. In case they have forgotten they are to report the news, not give their opinions or use their jobs to espouse a political platform - what a disgrace. Many have no compunction about outright lying - **when evil becomes good**.

I read news headlines online, then I can choose to believe it or not without having to listen to a mouthpiece blabber on and on; trying to tell me what I need to believe or understand. The unfortunate thing is we have a lot of idiots that don't have the common sense or intelligence to sort out what is true and what is not- **and they vote**. They very seldom report on heartwarming, moral, family happenings. It is all about tragedy, violence, backstabbing, drama; but it is all about money and those types of news reports are what seems to sell. I know I can go to the Christian Broadcasting Network and get truth and stories about real people who make a real difference.

The sports' commentators crack me up. Some have not even played the sport and they want to tell me what just happened in a particular play. If I am watching the game, I can see; I don't need a dissertation, especially from someone who has never played the sport and just has the job because they knew someone or because of their gender.

Oh, and Hollywood - when did acting qualify a person to become an expert on all topics. They want to rant and rave about sexual harassment and gun violence, yet they promote both in their promiscuous and violent films. Of course making a fool of themselves gets the media attention from the same media outlets that make fools of themselves.

Recently I read a quote from LeBron James where he said he would not shut up and dribble because "I mean too much to society". Really? When did playing basketball become a worthwhile contribution to society? It is entertainment. He also had the audacity to say that a lot of the people who voted for President Trump were probably uneducated. That comment came from someone with no higher level of learning and plays professional basketball. Wow, I really consider those people an authority on political statistics.

Many of the media are bullies. A big issue in elementary and secondary schools now is bullying. Class time is spent to teach students about bullying and the repercussions; but still bullying thrives, many times because of lack of school officials to address. Responsible parents teach their children that bullying is not acceptable, but yet adults in much of the news outlets are bullies. Calling people derogatory names and wishing bad things on them is bullying. So, why is it okay for adults to do such, but not minors - **when evil becomes good.**

I personally stay away from outlets like Facebook and Twitter because to me they are a gossip forum for people to badmouth someone they don't have the guts to talk to face to face. I do see how it can be a good advertising outlet for businesses. As with a lot of things, there are always those who abuse it. If you want to be my friend, you can call me, text me, or email me. I don't want my family's pictures plastered all over the web. The people that I care about seeing them has access to them.

"The Lord detests lying lips, but he delights in men who are truthful." Proverbs 12:22 (NIV)

TWENTY-ONE

Global Warming

Al Gore and a few others really sold the airheads a bill of goods; same concept as the person who came up with Common Core and suckered the schools into going with it. I guess the 1930s were having Global Warming also, recording the hottest temperatures on record. If that was Global Warming, then apparently it hasn't destroyed us in the last 88 years.

God is still in control. He controls everything in nature and in the universe. Granted, man has not and is not always a good steward of the environment and suffers negative side effects because of such. This is nothing new. However, the earth is not going to end by sunburn. This world will end by Satan's armies being defeated by God's army.

People make a lot of money off of shallow-minded amoebas who would believe that the world is actually flat if a liberal told them it was. And, these people vote. How many hundreds bought into Jim Jones' false teaching and drank the Kool-aid; and how many hundreds did the same with David Koresh and went to hell with him. Global Warming is the same hogwash.

I think Alfred Nobel would be flabbergasted to see the award named after him given to such people as Al Gore and Barak Obama. Giving them such an award rates the same as if it was given to the Mickey Mouse Clubhouse crew for their ability to do the Hotdog dance.

TWENTY-TWO

War

I am in no form or fashion an expert on war but I do know how God fought His sanctioned wars in the Bible, and it was not politically correct. I would say He is the Master Expert on war. If you will read the accounts of His sanctioned wars in the Old Testament, most of the time He instructed His people to leave nothing standing: men, women, children, animals, and material goods. I am not going to go into specific battles because if you are interested you can read for yourself the accounts in the Bible. You might say that was then and this is now; but as God states, He does not change. **See Malachi 3:6** The reasoning for destroying everything was quite simple. If you leave behind women and children, they will just rear up another generation of enemies.

I am not saying that all recent wars in which the United States has been involved were all God sanctioned, but I believe some of them were. I believe the Revolutionary War was God sanctioned. He was going to build a God-fearing nation. The Civil War was a travesty, pride got in the way and pitted brother against brother; but people suffer consequences for their sin. World War I and World War II destroyed evil empires much like the Babylonian and Assyrian empires were destroyed in the Old Testament. I applaud President Truman for the action he took to bring a final end to World War II. The Vietnam War unfortunately turned out to be a big mistake. It might have started out with the right intentions, but I believe this is the first war that we saw political correctness raise its ugly head. Whatever territory on which a war is fought, there will always be civilians that get caught in the crossfire. It is inevitable.

In Vietnam, the military were fighting an enemy that used civilians covertly, but yet some troops were punished for killing such. Nonsense. Thousands of lives were lost, but nothing was really accomplished. If the enemy was such a threat, the military should have gone in and wiped them out like they did in World War II. If not, they should not have gotten involved in the first place. The Vietnam War was my era. A lot of young men I went to school with were drafted as soon as they graduated out of high school. Most of these young men who were drafted probably didn't even know the reasoning behind the war, but they obeyed the law and went; and many did not make it back. But, then you had the cowards who skipped the country to avoid going. They used flimsy excuses. If they truly believed their excuse was legitimate, they should have stayed in the country and suffered the penalty. Those that skipped out should have lost their citizenship and all rights as a United States citizen. Many of the protestors treated our soldiers horrendously. Our soldiers were and are the heroes, they did the duty they were called to do by their government whether they agreed with it or not. The disrespectful protestors were and are still a disgrace for the way they treat these veterans.

Since that war we have had numerous "conflicts" and are currently engaged in warfare in numerous places. President Reagan handled Libya quite well. Iraq was a whole other story. A lot of lives were lost and what was really accomplished. We are still dealing with those people, just another generation; a good example of the principle I noted above about leaving people behind. The United States should have just gone in and made that whole area a parking lot and be done with it. If you are not willing to do that, you should never get involved. It has just escalated into many other areas, dealing with basically the same type of people. Fighting wars in a manner that is deemed politically correct is idiotic and destructive.

There is one final war yet to come, that is God's war, the Battle of Armageddon. God and His army will be the victors. It will not be a politically correct war. At the end of this war, there will not be much of a world population left. Women and children will not be spared. God is not politically correct. He is Righteous and Just, He is the Supreme Law and Leader of the Universe. He is still in control, and none can withstand Him.

TWENTY-THREE

Israel

Some might ask why I am including a section about Israel. The Hebrews/Israelites/Jews (For a study on these three distinctions, see my book "Understanding Israel and the Jews" available through Amazon and Barnes and Noble) have been an important part of history for thousands of years and they still are. The Israelites are God's chosen people. God told them in **Deuteronomy 7:6-8, "For thou art an holy people unto the Lord thy God: the LORD thy God hath chosen thee to be a special people unto himself, above all people that are upon the face of the earth. The Lord did not set his love upon you, nor choose you, because ye were more in number than any people; for ye were the fewest of all people: But because the Lord loves you, and because he would keep the oath which he had sworn unto your father, hath the Lord brought you out with a mighty hand and redeemed you out of the house of bondmen, from the hand of Pharaoh king of Egypt."(KJV)** God refers to Israel as the "apple of his eye" in **Zechariah 2:8.** God chose Abraham, a Hebrew, to be the Father of His many nations. Abraham's Grandson Jacob was the father of the Twelve Tribes of Israel through his twelve sons, from where descendants all over the world live today. God has not given up on Israel even though they rejected Christ when He came. He still has a plan and purpose for them today and they will come back into the fold at the end of days as is talked about in **Romans 11:26.**

One of the reasons that God has protected and looked favorably upon the United States is that for the most part we have been a friend to Israel. However, during the Obama Administration, that was in jeopardy. President Trump has reaffirmed our support of Israel and recognizing Jerusalem as its Capitol is definitely a step in the right direction; also moving the United States Embassy there. God is very clear in how He will deal with any nation/people who come against the "apple of His eye". In **Genesis 12:2&3, He says speaking to Abraham (still called Abram at this time), "And I will make of thee a great nation, and I will bless thee, and make thy name great; and thou shall be a blessing: And I will bless them that bless thee, and curse him that curseth thee..."(KJV)**

The Genesis Scripture is a warning to all of us. God never goes back on His promises. The Israelite people have suffered much through history, some of their own making in being disobedient to God, but some of that suffering because of evil people. According to Scripture, their suffering is not yet done, but woe to those nations and peoples that come against them. God's army will annihilate them. There is no nation in the world that can withstand God's army; and God and His army is coming to set things right.

Ideologies

TWENTY-FOUR

Capitalism vs Socialism

Socialism rewards those who don't work (I am not talking about retired people) and penalizes those that do. Welfare as I have described earlier is a Socialist program. Who said we all should have the same. The Declaration of Independence says that all of God's creation has the right to the "pursuit" of happiness. Pursuit means that you must do something, take action, not sit on your laurels and expect someone else to make you happy. Socialist programs like welfare take from the working man and woman through taxes and gives to those who do nothing for it. If they want to have a standard of living like the worker, then they need to get a job. Unfortunately, these assistance programs have made it more profitable for some to live off of the government than to get a job. Some have scruples and will work no matter the wage, but others don't have any shame in living off of the taxpayers. The only people that prosper under Socialism are the leaders of the government. They keep their money, while taking yours and controlling every aspect of your life. If you look at the history of Eastern Europe, you will see how well Socialism works. Not. Eventually a Socialist society will always collapse. An economy in such a society cannot endure. The leadership hoards their wealth, while the people live in poverty and misery, and do not do the kind of work necessary to sustain an economy.

Obamacare has come very close to being socialized medicine. It is a disaster. It was touted as a program that would provide medical insurance for everyone, what a joke.

Some people that had insurance before have none now because they can no longer afford it. Others still have it but have to pay higher premiums, me for one. Then for the powers that be to tell people they have to have some type of medical insurance or they will be fined; pretty socialist I would say. Who are the ones that have not suffered. Guess who: the young ones on Medicaid, not Seniors, who have never worked, get government assistance. Obamacare didn't impact them much. The quality and availability of services went South also. Medical care with these conglomerate hospitals have become big business, an assembly line of running people through like cattle. A doctor my husband had for 30+ years recently retired early because he refused to treat his patients like cattle. He had sold his practice to a conglomerate that had taken over the local hospital and he had agreed to stay on for a while. He did so until they told him he could not diagnose a patient with more than two things, had to refer them to a specialist; and told him he could not spend more than 15 minutes with each patient. Basically, he told them to take a hike, and retired. Unfortunately, the community lost a dedicated doctor who had spent many hours, day and night, tending to the needs of his patients. Kudos to him for not compromising his values.

If you look at the medical statistics for such counties as Canada and Great Britain who have socialized medicine, you will find substandard care. Cancer survivors are fewer in number than to those of the United States because of lack of care and waiting times to see doctors. Many people from those countries come to the United States to get the medical care they do not have the access to in their own countries. How much longer that will be the case, who knows. Healthcare is not a right, it is a privilege. The government needs to keep its nose out of it.

Capitalism on the other hand promotes hard work and competition. In a Socialist society there is no competition because everyone is getting the same whether they do anything or not, so why try to make things better. God has given each person a freewill to make choices. Some make good choices, some make bad. Some may have an easier start than others; but through grit and hard work, they can rise above those circumstances and excel. History is full of these success stories. No one ever has a legitimate excuse that the way they live is a result of their lack of opportunity. God gives each of us opportunities. What we do with those opportunities is our choice. A quote I read somewhere and since cannot find basically said that the only failure is doing nothing. People that do nothing and expect someone to make their lifestyle equal to the ones doing something are failures. Winston Churchill once said, "Socialism is a philosophy of failure, the creed of ignorance, and the gospel of envy, its inherent virtue is the equal sharing of misery." A key word in this quote is envy. Many anti-Capitalists are just plain jealous. **Proverbs 14:30 says, "A sound heart is the life of the flesh: but envy the rottenness of the bones."(KJV)** I don't begrudge the Walton family, or the Gates family, or the Trump family, or any such family of their great wealth. Some have worked very hard to get where they are, others have inherited and are maintaining that wealth. Some will argue that it was gotten by corrupt means. If that be the case, then at some point they will be held accountable by the Supreme Law of the land, God, even if it doesn't happen in this life. I like the fact that I have opportunities to be what I can be, what God has created me to be, not what some greedy, power seeking government tells me what I am to be.

Consider the parable in **Matthew 25:14-30**. Jesus is telling the parable. He tells of a master who gives three of his servants each different amounts of money to handle for him while he goes on a journey. When the master comes back, the two he gave the most to had invested the money and made more money for the master. The one who had gotten the least, did nothing with his. He was lazy and then tried to make an excuse to the master as to why he had not increased what he had been given. The master's reply was "You wicked and lazy and idle servant! Did you indeed know that I reap where I have not sowed and gather [grain] where I have not winnowed? Then you should have invested my money with the bankers and at my coming I would have received what was my own with interest. So take the talent away from him and give it to the one who has the ten [most] talents. For to everyone who has will more be given, and he will be furnished richly so that he will have an abundance, but from the one who does not have, even what he does have will be taken away. And throw the good-for-nothing servant into the outer darkness; there will be weeping and grinding of teeth." **(AMPC)** God is a Capitalist.

TWENTY-FIVE

Liberalism

Liberalism as we know it today is man ignoring the basic Laws of God and making laws to justify his own depraved way of thinking. It is an unholy train of thought and is contributing to the downfall of this nation.

Illinois is a prime example of what happens to a state that is ruled by liberal leaders. Illinois is broke, is corrupt, and has two cities with the highest crime rates in the country; one of which is number one. As of June 2017, Illinois had the poorest credit rating on record of any state in the United States. Downstate Illinois is conservative and votes conservatively; all except East St. Louis and Cairo. However, our votes cannot override the liberal Chicago. As of this writing, we have two liberal senators and a governor that might as well be a Democrat. Currently the Mayor of Chicago is Rahm Emanuel, do I need to say more. Chicago is in the top 30 cities for crime and has some of the strictest gun laws; but restricting gun ownership is supposed to improve this - right. You believe that, then I have some property in the Everglades to sell you. Taxpayers fund abortions, the state has more people on welfare than are employed, and is the largest user of Food Stamps in the Midwest. The state also has some of the highest property taxes in the country. In 2016 Illinois had the most outbound people in the country. Because of high taxes, companies like Motorola, Kraft, and General Mills have either moved plants to other states or greatly cut their workforce in the state; so much for what liberal leadership does for you. If I had my druthers, I would recommend downstate split off and become a part of Missouri, let East St. Louis, Cairo, and the Chicago area fend for themselves.

California is another example of what liberal leaders and thinking does for you. According to an article in the January 2018 Los Angeles Times, California is the poverty capital of America. According to the San Diego Tribune in an article in 2012, California only has 12% of the population in the country, but has 34% on welfare rolls. I imagine their population and welfare rolls have increased now with all of the illegal immigrants they harbor. Like Illinois, California is also starting to see an exodus of its people. When they are only left with their illegal immigrants and liberal Hollywood, we will see how long they will last. When some in the state were talking about leaving the country because they do not like President Trump; I said yeah! don't let the door hit you in the arse. But, like Alec Baldwin was going to leave if Bush was elected, they are still here.

TWENTY-SIX

Politically Correct Language

Calling a spade a spade means to tell it like it is. Whoa! Was that cliche racist, not politically correct? It was okay until recently when some pseudointellectual decided it might be racist, the kind of people who have nothing better to do with their time than come up with such things. In case anyone is interested in the origin of this saying, look it up. I will not waste my time explaining it.

The term for black people has changed at least four times in my lifetime thus far. I am not for sure what is considered to be the politically correct term at present, and I really don't care. I refer to them as black people. When I was a child in the 50s and early 60s, the term was colored or Negro. Oops that makes it five changes. I grew up in a very small Midwestern town where no Black people lived. The closest Black population was 25 miles away. Children are always curious when they see something different and sometimes make comments that will embarrass their parents. I can remember as a child my first memory of going to this town 25 miles away. My mother told me that I would probably see people that were a different color than we were, dark skinned; but that God had created them too and they were the same as us, just a different skin color. I was not to make any comments about it. I never in my whole childhood ever heard my parents make derogatory comments about any other race. The term then went to Black, then to African American, then to a person of color. I asked my grandson one time when he was in first grade how they referred to Blacks. He said they were called people with brown skin. Later when they had an influx of Hispanics, I asked if they referred to them as brown skin people. He said they were brown skin people and now the previous brown skin people were referred to as black. Hmm.

Indians are now Native Americans which the term actually does them honor because they are really the group that can claim first property rights to this country which was stolen away from them by many European groups. However, different theories have circulated that the Native Americans as we know them were not the first inhabitants of the Americas; but it is pretty much all circumstantial. Some colleges that have had different Indian symbols as mascots have since gotten rid of them because it is not considered politically correct, and racist. I have not kept up with all of that business but in some cases I would think it would be an honor, but I can see how it could be degrading depending on how the symbol is represented. There are Asian Indians and then there are American Indians, quite distinctive.

It would be nice if people just referred to themselves as Americans if they are citizens of this country. Why should it make a difference what nationality or race you are. When I travel if someone asks me where I am from, I don't say I am an English/Irish American living in the Midwest. On job applications they group all of us European descent people into the Caucasian category. I could take offense at that. Maybe I don't want to be included with the Swedes and Germans, not so, but my point is why does that make a difference. In some cases, I know, it is for affirmative action purposes. However, I am not aware that the Asians get special treatment. I know some people from such countries as Spain and Argentina have a problem being grouped into the same category as Mexicans, because they are all considered Hispanic.

It is not queer anymore, it is gay or lesbian. I guess the term homosexual is out also. According to some if I am against this type of lifestyle, I am homophobic. A phobia is a fear and I sure am not afraid of those who choose the homosexual lifestyle. I just know it is a sin and God condemns it. They have freewill and they make the choice. The initial origin of the word bi meant two or twice, but it is now used with the word sexual and means someone who swings both ways. Oh, excuse me, you are bisexual not lesbian. Glad you clarified that difference for me. I thought if you are female and swing both ways you are both bisexual and lesbian; and if you are male and swing both ways you are both bisexual and gay. But, then on the other hand, maybe you are all gay. LBGT - **when evil becomes good**.

When a spouse decides to sleep around with someone else besides their spouse, no it is not an extramarital affair. It is adultery, it is sin. When you choose to have multiple sex partners whether you are married or not, you are whoring around. At one time God called His people whores because they were going after strange gods.

I just read a quote which said, "Calling an illegal immigrant an undocumented immigrant is like calling a meth dealer an undocumented pharmacist". Sorry, it did not list the author of the quote. Here are a few of the politically correct terms. People are no longer deaf, they are hearing impaired. They are no longer blind, they are seeing impaired. They are not retarded, down syndrome, insane; they are mentally challenged. The person is not the garbage collector, he is a sanitation engineer. Oh, I must say he or she, man or he can no longer be used as all encompassing. Anyhow, they engineer the garbage/trash. If the right wing protests, it is a riot; if the left wing riots, it is a protest. A terrorist is a freedom fighter. Global warming is climate change. Instead of having a broken home, it is dysfunctional. My broken watch is dysfunctional. When I take it to the jeweler, I will ask him to mechanically engineer my dysfunctional watch. We no longer have housewives, we have domestic engineers. I liked being a wife in the house when my children were little, who wants to be a tame mechanic. If you decide to become a male instead of a female, it is not a sex change, you have had gender reassignment. In God's eyes, you are still a male, a "dysfunctional" one. If you disagree with the far left, you are either a racist, a Nazi, or a Fascist. If you are very conservative, you are on the terror watch list and called homophobic. Instead of a criminal being wanted, they are a person of interest. All those words that end in man like Fireman, have had the man changed to something else that will include either male or female. It is no longer a blackboard, but a chalkboard even though many of them still are the color black. I am surprised we still have the color black in the crayon box. The crayon box must be racist, but it does seem to get along with the reds, blues, browns, greens, and so on. However, we do have colors now like vermillion and mauve. We must give every shade a distinction. Oh, a big pet peeve of mine - Seasons Greetings instead of Merry Christmas. Guess what folks, if you have a problem with the Christ attached to the mas, then work on that holiday. You can take off another day. This one was a new one on me. It is not proper to call it a flip chart. It is an easel because the word flip is a derogatory term for Filipinos. You are no longer fat, you are obese; or like the Ewe in the picture: "Ewes not fat, ewes just fluffy." Well, I am fluffy because my fat index is too high. There are plenty more, but someone was paid way too much money to come up with all of these terms. It goes back to, "just call a spade a spade".

TWENTY-SEVEN

Politically Correct History

Now we have some trying to erase history by tearing down monuments, how ridiculous. History is history, we should learn from our history and try not to make the same mistakes. Monuments have different meanings for different people. We should never worship a monument anyhow, so if you don't like the monument or what it stands for, don't look at it. Just like one person can look at a piece of art and see something different than another person looking at it, so one monument can be a lesson learned for someone and an offense to someone else. I spend extended periods of time each year in the New Orleans area. It is a shame they have torn down some of their historical monuments that have been here decades just to satisfy a small group of people that think everything should revolve around them. Some people still agree with the Confederacy while others are offended by what it stood for, but it is each group's freedom to do so.

Some have tried to erase what happened to the Jews in Germany during the 1930s and 1940s, wanting people to believe it never happened. Incidences like these should continue to be taught in history classes to let our young ones know about evil in the world. Teaching Jesus Christ in public schools is not allowed, but some have started teaching the doctrines of Islam. Evolution has been taught for years, but not creation.

Jesus Christ was crucified for man's sins , Malcolm X was a radical Muslim who promoted violence, African tribes sold their own people into slavery because they wanted to weed out the ones they thought were inferior...are these historical facts taught students in the history books?

TWENTY-EIGHT

Christianity

I gave Christianity its own chapter because Christianity is not religiosity, it is a relationship. True Christianity is not about manmade doctrine. It is the Law of God through Jesus Christ His Son. It requires each individual to have their own personal relationship with Jesus Christ, making Him Lord of their lives. It is not based on good works or what society deems as a "good" person. Many polls will identify a large percentage of people as Christians, when in fact they are not. Christians are actually in the minority. People will identify themselves as Christians just because they believe there is a God. There is a reason the word Christ is in Christian, it goes back to the relationship I described above. Knowing there is a God and there is Jesus Christ does not make one a Christian. Satan knows that. Believing is putting one's total trust and faith in Jesus Christ. It is not head knowledge, it is a heart relationship.

As I mentioned earlier, many groups today seem to think the religion clause of the Constitution applies to every religion except Christianity. They also seem to conveniently overlook the part about free exercise. It is okay for a Mosque to blare their call to prayer all over the neighborhood and even have streets (government property) blocked off for their rituals, but some communities forbid people to have Bible Studies in their homes. Christian business owners (who also own the property on which the business is) are prosecuted because they refuse to cater to people who want them to do something that goes against their belief - **when evil becomes good.**

In Conclusion

TWENTY-NINE

When Evil Becomes Good

Most parents I hope teach their children that it is wrong to lie. However, that principle seems to be "do as I say, not as I do". Most of the news you cannot believe. In the past it was only the tabloids that earned this distinction, but now the major news media are a bunch of liars. It is not fake news, it is lies. Government officials look us in the eye and lie. Putting a spin on news, embellishing it; whatever term you want to use, it is lying. But, to the general public, it does not seem to be a big deal; they seem to have become hardened to it...**when evil becomes good.**

We used to hear a lot about hate language. The only time now we seem to hear the term hate language used is if a white person says something derogatory about some other race, or if a person says something derogatory about an "alternative" lifestyle. But, it is not hate language for liberals to say hateful things about Christians, or people to use violent language against the President. It used to be that if even a veiled threat was made against the President, the person would be arrested. I remember in the late 1960s a young man I had gone to school with made a comment in a bar about killing the president. He was arrested and not heard from again. The rumor was he ended up in a mental institution. How many threats and derogatory words have been used against President Trump and nothing done, i.e., Hollywood idiots, among others...**when evil becomes good.**

The victim mentality - many want to be the victim to excuse their bad behavior rather than take responsibility for their actions, and our society has bought into it. When did the cop become the evil one and the criminal become the poor innocent soul who never had a chance. When did the illegal immigrant become the victim rather than the law breaker. When did the addict become the victim rather than the end product of bad choices. When did a weapon become the cause of the killing rather than the person using the weapon. When did the killer become the victim of mental illness rather than just calling a spade a spade and recognizing that there are evil people...**when evil becomes good.**

The blame game - it is everyone else's fault a political candidate lost, not that the public realized the person was a liar and a loser. The criminal is not at fault for his/her behavior because they were abused as a child, they were raised in the projects, they are the wrong color. Every person has choices, some make good ones, some bad ones. Every person is given opportunities. They can either grab hold of the opportunities given, or play the victim all their life and become a nonproductive leech on society...**when evil becomes good.**

When did it become a crime to be cruel to an animal, but okay to kill an unborn child. When did it become okay for a man to have sex with a man and a woman to have sex with a woman, but a crime for a 20-yr old man to have sex with a 16-yr old; yet a 12-yr old can be tried as an adult. When did it become okay for a court to tell parents what type of medical treatment they have to have for their child or they have to allow their child to become a girl even though they were born a boy...**when evil becomes good.**

THIRTY

Sin

Sin is a word that our society hardly ever mentions. Even many churches don't use the word anymore. It is not "politically correct", it might hurt someone's feelings, it might show intolerance. Sin is disobedience to God. God is not politically correct. He is not tolerant. He is longsuffering. There is a difference between tolerance and longsuffering. Tolerance is accepting one's behavior, longsuffering is giving one a good amount of time to change their behavior before judgment is rendered. God is narrow minded. In **John 14:6 (Jesus says), " I am the way, the truth, and the life, no man cometh unto the Father except by me." (KJV)** God does not change with time, His Word is as applicable today as it was thousands of years ago. **Malachi 3:6 says, "For I am the Lord, I change not..." (KJV)** Man's laws do not supercede God's laws. Any action or thought that does not line up with the Word of God is Sin.

Matthew 24:37 talks about the days of Noah. For those of you who are not familiar with God's Word, society in the days of Noah was quite like what is going on in ours today. It was very decadent, as was in the cities of Sodom and Gomorrah. All kinds of sexual sin was rampant: homosexuality, incest, bestiality, every kind of fornication imaginable. God completely destroyed Sodom and Gomorrah except for Lot and his family because Lot was Abrahams's nephew. God spared him for Abraham's sake. Everything on earth was destroyed in Noah's time except for Noah and his family and the animals he took on the ark. Noah a was righteous man in God's eyes. Noah tried to get the people to see the error of their ways, but they laughed at him. These were societies where every kind of sin was rampant, and they were very chaotic. God gave them plenty of time to change their ways, but they mocked God by ignoring him. Not much looks different in our society today. Incest is not legal, but it is not rare. Many times people look the other way. Bestiality does happen also. It hasn't been that long since homosexuality was illegal, but now it is praised. Corrupt governments barely get a blink, lying is a way of life, life is not really sacred unless it is an animal's, white collar theft seems to be more tolerated than other kinds, and perverted lifestyles are just alternatives.

Instead of sin being sin, there is always an excuse, a victim of something. Where there is sin, there is darkness. It is ironic that the lighting in extremely violent or graphic sexual scenes in many movies are darkened compared to other scenes. Satan is the ruler of darkness. When a society becomes more liberal, violating God's laws, it will become darker and reap more devastating consequences. The rise of more sexual permissiveness brings on less respect for each other and results in a rise in: sex trafficking, sexually transmitted diseases such as HIV, incest, adultery, and divorce. Marriage in many arenas is no longer sacred, no longer a lifetime commitment, no longer a precursor to sexual relations; disposable. The darkness resulting from societal permissiveness also results in more darkness in individual lives. Darkness brings with it mental illnesses, a search for satisfaction in such things as drugs which brings with it an increase in suicides. It has a spiraling effect.

When it is okay to murder the unborn, life begins to take on less meaning in other areas of life also. When there is no longer a sanctity of life, rapes increase, espousal abuse increases, other murders increase. There is no longer a respect for life in any form or fashion.

When the good guy suddenly becomes the bad guy; and the bad guy becomes the victim, crime becomes the norm. People's hearts become hardened to the bad, they become pawns for Satan's deceits.

Sin entered the world in the Garden. God gave man a freewill to make choices. When Eve allowed herself to be deceived by Satan and Adam followed suit, sin entered. The bloodline was contaminated. We are all descendants of Adam and Eve; thus, we all have contaminated blood. Each human being is born with contaminated blood - sin. Does that give us an excuse to say that we are not accountable for sin because we were born sinners. No, we have a choice. God always gives us a choice. We can either obey or not. People are not born homosexual, they are not born a female in a man's body. They make choices. We can either choose to continue to live a life of sin and suffer the damnation of hell in the next life; or we can choose the option that God gives us: choosing His Son Jesus Christ as our personal Lord and Savior, and spending our eternity in Heaven with Him instead of in Hell with Satan. We either serve God or Satan. There is no other choice and there are not many ways to God; only through Jesus Christ. Jesus is the only light that can penetrate the darkness of this world.

Romans 1:21 (AMP) "They knew God [as Creator], they did not honor Him as God or give thanks [for His wondrous creation]. On the contrary, they became worthless in their thinking [godless, with pointless reasonings, and silly speculations], and their foolish heart was darkened."

Many recognize God as Creator and many don't; but whether they do or not, there are many who do not honor Him. Like the Romans Scripture says, we have many today that are worthless in their thinking, have stupid reasonings, and are foolish. Does this remind you of many of our political leaders, Hollywood people, and professional athletes? **I Corinthians 1:27 (AMP)** says "But God has selected [for His purpose] the foolish things of the world to shame the wise [revealing their ignorance], and God has selected [for His purpose] the weak things of the world to shame the things which are strong [revealing their frailty]." Those that do not have that relationship with God through Jesus Christ cannot understand the things of God, the wise and mighty things; they only have wisdom and understanding in their own mind. Everyday in some form or fashion, we hear from some of these foolish, darkened minds. They live in a dark world within themselves because they do not have true wisdom and understanding.

John 3:19 (Jesus speaking) - "And this is the condemnation, that light is come into the world, and men loved darkness rather than light, because their deeds were evil." **(KJV)** The light was and is Jesus Christ. Many love their sinful lifestyles and live in darkness. They prefer to stay in darkness because the light will reveal their evil.

II Corinthians 4:4 - "In whom the god of this world hath blinded, the minds of them which believe not, lest the light of the glorious gospel of Christ, who is the image of God, should shine unto them."**(KJV)** Satan is the god of this world and master of those who do not have Jesus Christ as their Lord and Savior. He wants to continue to be their master so he blinds them to the truth of the Gospel because if they ever search out the Truth, the Light of Jesus Christ will transform them from darkness into light.

Ephesians 4:18 (NIV) - "They are darkened in their understanding and separated from the life of God because of the ignorance that is in them due to the hardening of their hearts." The longer people reject the truth of Jesus Christ the harder their hearts become and the less likely they are to ever accept the Truth; thus, the more ignorant they become and greater is the darkness in their lives.

Psalms 82:5 (AMP) - "The rulers do not know nor do they understand; They walk on in the darkness [of complacent satisfaction]; All the foundations of the earth [the fundamental principles of the administration of justice] are shaken." Many of our leaders walk in Satan's darkness, ignorant, deceived by Satan's deceit, assuming that their lives and this world will continue as is. Because of their worldly ignorance, the all important foundations of our society erode.

Much of the world in which we live today focuses on self. People are taught to take care of number one first. We live in a very self-centered society. Jesus taught just the opposite. We are to esteem others above ourselves; we are to put others' needs before ours. Jesus Himself told His disciples that He came to serve. Too many today are concerned about only one thing, what's in it for me.

As long as this nation, this world, these people have breath, there is hope; but the only hope is through Jesus Christ. People worry about nuclear war, they worry about "global warming", they worry about an economic crash, they worry about death. Only those that do not know Christ have reason to worry. Yes, the end will come, but the children of God have nothing to fear. I want to clarify who are the children of God. God is the creator of every human being, but they are not all His children. As I noted earlier, sin entered the world in the Garden. When sin entered, man was separated from God. We are born sinners. God is a righteous and just God. He cannot tolerate sin. Does He love all of us? Yes, but He will not excuse sin. Christ was the one time sacrifice who took on the world's sin to atone for us so that continual sacrifices would not have to be offered as was the case before Christ. However, Christ's sacrifice only applies to those who put their trust and faith in Him, make Him Lord of their Life - these are the children of God.

As I mentioned before, the Bible talks about when evil becomes good and good becomes evil. Political Correctness has contributed to such. God's children know what the end will be. We know that wars will increase, evil will thrive, and the world will become darker and darker; but the child of God has nothing to fear. Those that refuse to take advantage of the Hope before they take their last breath will go into eternal damnation, the everlasting fire of torment. We, the children of God, will move from this life into an eternal life with God, more amazing and beautiful than any human mind can ever imagine.

Yes, it is frustrating to me to see such sin around me. Am I a perfect person; no, but I try to pattern my life after Jesus and I do not live a lifestyle of sin. I feel sadness for those that continue to live their sinful lifestyles as if there is no day of reckoning, because I know what their end shall be. I would never wish eternal damnation on anyone, no matter how bad society deems them to be. The vilest person can be changed by the blood of Jesus Christ. I feel sadness for this nation of the United States because I know how many sacrifices men and women made to make it a great nation, "one nation under God". We were never meant to be a nation of diversity. The word diversity comes from a root meaning to divide. We were to be a nation of united people under God, the Supreme Law of the land.

Mark 3:25 (Jesus speaking) (KJV) - "And if a house be divided against itself, that house cannot stand." - As many of you know President Lincoln used that quote. Some of you probably thought that quote was from him, when actually it comes from the Bible. Diversity in our society has been touted as a great thing, but actually it has divided this nation. President Lincoln knew this to be true. He knew that if there continued to be a North and a South, the United States of America would fall. The United States is probably more divided now than it has ever been in history. In reality we are no longer united states. There are so many different fractions and factions causing division, not unity. At least the North and the South had two unified parts for the most part. We don't even have that now. The so-called distinct groups are so divided within themselves they cannot even get along. This nation is on very shaky ground. However, because of God's children humbling themselves before Him and praying, He has given us another season. How long this season will be, we do not know; but we must make the most of the time He has given us to reach others for Him.

How the United States will fall out in the scheme of things mentioned in the Book of Revelation remains to be seen. There are many different ideas on what her part will be; will she be overcome, or will she be one of the ten mentioned.

Her only hope is to turn back to God and recognize that He is the Supreme Power.

Evil will never win out. God is still in control, He is not being blind sided. He is not surprised. When He is ready in His perfect timing, the ax will fall. Judgment is coming and no one will escape it.

When evil was good...evil will no longer exist, sin will be eradicated forever. Amen!!!

www.ingramcontent.com/pod-product-compliance
Lightning Source LLC
Chambersburg PA
CBHW050649250726
48662CB00002B/575